Cyber Citizenship and Cyber Safety™

Cyber Literacy
Evaluating the Reliability of Data

Susan Regan Gregson

rosen publishing's
rosen
central®

New York

We would like to thank Laura Gurak, author of Cyberliteracy: Navigating the Internet with Awareness, which was the first published work to coin the term "cyberliteracy."

Published in 2008 by The Rosen Publishing Group, Inc.
29 East 21st Street, New York, NY 10010

Library of Congress Cataloging-in-Publication Data

Gregson, Susan R.
Cyber literacy: evaluating the reliability of data / Susan Regan Gregson.
    p. cm.—(Cyber citizenship and cyber safety)
Includes bibliographical references.
ISBN-13: 978-1-4042-1353-1 (lib. bdg.)
1. Electronic information resource literacy—Juvenile literature.
2. Computer network resources—Evaluation—Juvenile literature.
3. Internet and teenagers—Juvenile literature. I. Title.
ZA4065.G74 2007
025.04—dc22

                                                       2007029668

Manufactured in Malaysia

Contents

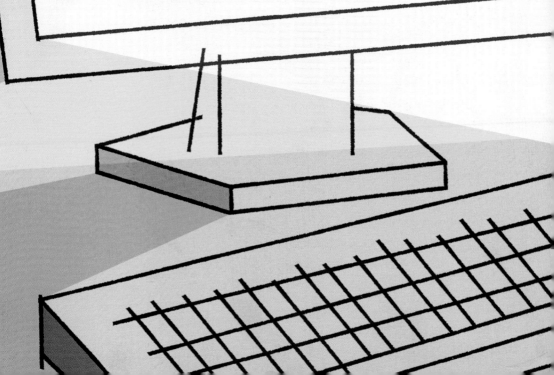

Introduction
Round and Round the World Wide Web We Go

In 1989, people all over the world received an e-mail about Craig Shergold. He was a nine-year-old boy in England with a brain tumor. His family expected him to die. Before he died, though, Craig wanted to get into the *Guinness Book of World Records* so that his memory would live on forever. He told his family that he wanted to collect so many greeting and get-well cards that he broke the world record. They sent an e-mail to family and friends. Those family and friends sent an e-mail to their family and friends. Before long, the e-mail was traveling around the globe, from computer to computer. Craig was thrilled.

Over the course of the next year, people mailed sixteen million cards to Craig Shergold. He broke the world record by a long shot! Even better, he was still alive and doctors thought they might be able to operate on his brain tumor. In 1991, doctors successfully removed the tumor. Unfortunately, Craig and his family could not stop the greeting cards. By 1992, Craig had received thirty-three million cards to help him break a record he had already broken. The cards came to his home in England and to the children's Make-a-Wish Foundation in Atlanta, Georgia. Someone had changed the e-mail, telling readers to mail cards to Make-a-Wish.

Shergold, Shelford, Stafford: Oh My!

Somewhere along the way, the e-mail began to take on a life of its own. People changed the wording of the message. Craig Shergold became Craig Shelford and Craig Stafford. Some e-mails called him Craig Sheppard and Greg Sherwood. Although the names were a little different, the cards kept coming to the Make-A-Wish headquarters in Atlanta and to the Shergold family in England. So many cards had arrived that the Guinness World Record people ended the greeting card record category in 1992. Craig's thirty-three million cards will stand forever as the Guinness record.

The Make-a-Wish Foundation put a notice on its Web site saying it had never been involved in the request. It asked people to stop sending the cards. It even set up a toll-free

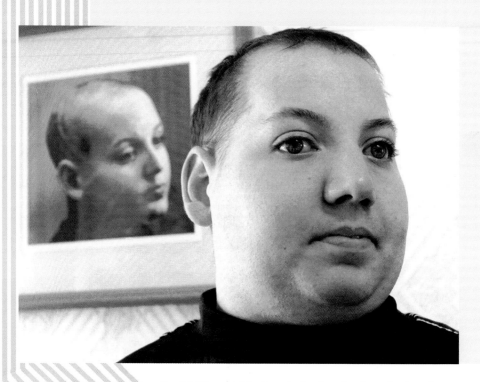

Craig Shergold stands in front of a photo of himself taken after his first cancer operation. Now cancer-free, Shergold received more than 250 million get-well cards because of e-mails that circled the globe for years, long after he was cured.

telephone hotline with a recorded message, asking, "Please stop sending cards. Feel free to send donations instead." The Guinness staff posted a notice on their own Web site telling readers that Craig was healthy and that the record for most items received in the mail was his. Craig and his family did interviews with the media. They begged people to stop mailing things to Craig. They told the world that any e-mail they received now was a hoax. In fact, all sorts of e-mails were traveling around the world now with stories of dying children who wanted to break a record. Nearly all of them were hoaxes.

Craig Shergold is a healthy young man today, but sometimes people still open their e-mail accounts and find a plea for cards from a boy dying of cancer. In fact, since Craig's first message, dozens of e-mails about other children have appeared. Some of the messages are completely false; the person and the hospital don't even exist. Other e-mails talk about real people who are ill but don't ask for cards. Why do people forward this kind of e-mail? Mostly because they received it from someone they know, and the story tugs at their hearts. But, that is just what it is: a story. Stories are not always true. We can do more harm than good if we rely on false information.

Cyber Literacy to the Rescue

When people know how to evaluate whether or not something they read is true, they are being literate. They know how to read and how to interpret what they read. They also know how to tell if information is correct and reliable. They can express in their own way what they read and learn and still keep the information accurate. If people can do this with online information, we say that they are cyber literate.

Cyber literacy is not just knowing how to use a computer and surf the Internet. It's about understanding the strengths and weaknesses of online information. Cyber literacy is knowing what is accurate and what is inaccurate in e-mails and on Web sites. It is also knowing how to use and credit online information in your own work.

People who read hoax e-mails or inaccurate information on the Internet and then pass that information along as true are not being cyber literate. They do not take the time or have the skill to figure out whether the information is reliable. You will not succeed in real life or online if you are not literate and cyber literate. Sending someone 200 million cards is a waste of time, money, and energy for a lot of people. Learning to be cyber literate will help you find and use accurate information.

Chapter 1

The Truth, the Whole Truth, and Nothing but the Truth?

What we know as the Internet and World Wide Web today began in the 1960s as three computers in California and Massachusetts. The United States Department of Defense needed to link the computers, but first someone had to figure out how to get them to communicate with each other. Soon there were more than 200 different computer networks. Universities and government agencies used the networks mostly for research. No one was allowed to use the Internet for commercial reasons. The networks combined into a larger network in 1974. It was called the "Internet." During the 1980s, other countries joined the Internet. In the late 1980s, commercial companies started providing access to the Internet. These companies were called Internet service providers, or ISPs.

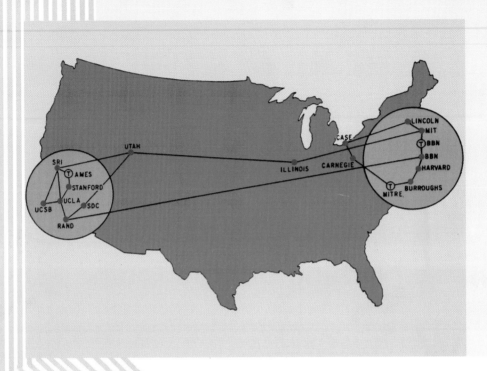

This 1971 map of the United States shows the very first links between computers. This network grew into the Internet we know today. You can find this image at www.cybergeography.org in the historical maps section.

In the 1990s, the commercial part of the Internet exploded. As more and more people signed up with ISPs to get on the Internet, the price came down. Lower costs allowed even more access to the Net. Browsers started to appear early in the 1990s, allowing people to easily get on the Internet and move around. They helped to organize all the information on the Web. Using a browser, people were able to visit Web pages and Web sites. Each document or file on the Web had its own address, or URL (uniform resource locator). One of the first browsers was named ViolaWWW, and the World Wide Web (WWW) was born.

Browsing the Web

A man uses wireless WiFi in a café in San Francisco to surf the Web and check his e-mail. More than 1.1 billion people around the world use the Internet.

Today, more than 1.1 billion people worldwide use the Internet, according to an online report posted in June 2007. In North America, 70 percent of people go online. There are many browsers to help people access the Web and all the information that it provides. Along with the Web, there are also other popular parts of the Internet. One of them is e-mail.

The computer is the hardware that uses software, or computer programs, to bring the Internet, Web, and e-mail

Itsy, Bitsy Spider

Search engines are computer programs that help you find information on the Web. Americans did more than seven billion online searches in May of 2007.

Search engines use little software robots called spiders to find information. The spiders "crawl" the Web to find and list words. The busy spiders build lists of keywords and where they found the words.

People use meta tags on their pages to give the spiders information about the page. A meta tag is a special way of coding information using hypertext markup language (HTML).

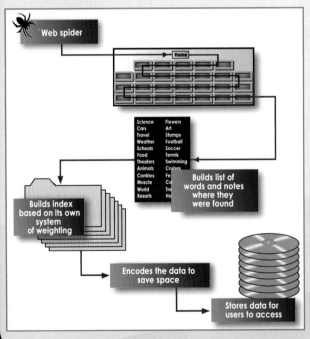

This chart shows how spiders crawl the Web for information. Spiders store data in a Web browser. People use browsers to find pages on the Web. You can find this chart at www.howstuffworks.com/search-engine1.htm.

Hypertext is a computer language that describes how a Web page should be formatted. Spiders speak HTML well! Meta tags tell the spiders which keywords and ideas on the page the spider should index, or store and rank. Based on how important, useful, and popular the page's words and ideas are, the spiders rank the page in a list.

Spiders index and store the data they find. When you type words into your search box, the search engine searches the index the spiders made. Pages pop up in a ranked list for you, based on the keywords you typed. Without spiders constantly crawling the Web, you would never be able to quickly find the information you need.

into millions of North American homes, schools, and businesses. The Web is literally hundreds of millions of URLs with billions of bytes of information. Fortunately, we have search engines to help us wade through the sea of information.

You can type words into a search engine and hit "submit" or "return," and a list of Web sites will appear. The words you typed are used in each of these sites. You might get thousands of hits, or Web sites, back from your search. You need to look at the few lines of information for each site that appear on the search engine list and select the best sites. Once you go to a Web site, you need to make sure it is accurate and looks professional, and that the data make sense. You can always return to your search list to find another site if the one you looked at isn't the right one for you.

Just How Smart Is That Friend of Yours, Anyway?

Just because teens are spending a lot of time online doesn't mean they are cyber literate. In fact, the opposite might be true. Some students steal the work of others and turn it in to teachers as their own. The Internet makes it a lot easier to find things to plagiarize, or use without credit. Teens and adults forward countless hoax e-mails, without checking out the facts first. Teens are more likely to pass along information that they read on popular Web sites. Some of these Web sites belong to companies advertising a product. Others belong to people writing their opinions. It is very easy, and dangerous, to take an opinion and treat it as a fact. There are thousands of Web pages full of false data. Others are called hate sites. People say bad things about a person or group on purpose and present the information as accurate.

Computers and the Web have become like a friend you hang out with after school. And like a flesh-and-blood friend, what the computer tells you is sometimes true, sometimes not. A computer doesn't grin and say, "just kidding," though. Teens and tweens, kids ages eleven and twelve, need to learn when to take their friend, the computer, at its word, and when to dig a little deeper. You also need to know when online information is so unreliable that it is harmful, such as a Web site supporting anorexia or suicide. Sometimes checking out the info on a Web site is as simple as talking to a parent, teacher, or librarian. Other times, you might need to read more Web sites, books, magazines, and journal articles.

This is especially true when you are working on a school report at the last minute. It's tempting to just use the information from one Web site and move on. Even if you wait until the middle of the night to do a report due the next day, you can still do things to make sure you find accurate information. You want to learn how to tell which Web sites are more reliable, or authoritative. This is also a part of cyber literacy.

Just like you wouldn't ask a friend, even a best friend, how to treat that ugly rash under your armpit, there are some Web sites you shouldn't use for report information. Dr. Laura Gurak from the University of Minnesota says in her book *Cyberliteracy* that "a cyberliterate citizen is one who knows how to be critical about online information." In this case, being critical doesn't mean that you don't like what you see. It means knowing how to evaluate the information, knowing what is accurate and what is not.

The Good, the Bad, the Totally Untrue

There are two main places to find online information: on the Web and in e-mail messages. Just how reliable is the information you find on a Web site? That depends on the background and knowledge of the person who created the Web site. Can you trust the information a friend sends you in an e-mail? That depends on where your friend found that information. Let's look at Web sites first.

Some sites are more accurate and reliable than others, based on the background of the site's creator. Anyone can put information on the Web. On one hand, that is good because it makes a lot of information available. On the other hand, that's not so good because it makes a lot of information available. Much of the information on the Web is false, incorrect, even harmful. If you want to be entertained, there are plenty of Web sites that are good for a laugh. They aren't meant to be taken seriously, though. Other sites have misleading information because the people who created the pages don't know the right things about a topic, even though they want you to think they do. Other Web sites may intentionally provide hateful, angry, or false views on people and issues. Some of these sites are hard to spot at first because they can look very professional.

If you are looking for data to use in a school report, though, you want to read sites put on the Web by people and organizations that are authorities, or experts, on the topic. When you are trying to form your own opinions about something, you want to make sure you read the right information, too. If you play baseball and want to lift weights to make your arms stronger, do you really want to take advice from some guy in Bora Bora who has never seen a bat, baseball, or free weight?

Searching the Web for Information

Suppose you are eleven years old and you just made the Little League baseball team. Your friend Will is on the team and has the highest batting average. You ask him how he gets so many hits. He tells you that he lifts weights to make his arms strong. You tell your dad that you want to lift weights. He tells you that he thinks that you are too young and will hurt your growing bones. You don't want to believe your dad

Smart people get their information from reliable Web sites. This screenshot is from the University of Chicago Comer Children's Hospital. The Web page has reliable information on how the hospital helps children with sports injuries.

because Will lifts weights and you want an awesome batting average, too. You boot up the family computer and start to surf the Web.

You go to your favorite search engine, type "weight lifting" and "children" in the search box, and hit "enter." Bam! You have a list of Web sites that might or might not talk about whether or not an eleven-year-old should lift weights. Sure, you might browse pages until you find one that says anyone can lift weights. Your dad isn't going to buy it, though, unless the information comes from a Web site that is reliable and authoritative. You scan some of the pages.

The easiest thing to keep in mind is that, just like real life, someone with experience in weight lifting and the health of kids will probably have the most reliable information. That pretty much rules out the site by the twenty-year-old "muscle head" in Bora Bora who thinks anyone can lift weights because he's been doing it since he was eight. He could be right, but there are other Web sites that are more likely to be right. You want to find those.

You might need to go back to your search list and look for who created the pages on the list. Look for coach associations, the Little League site, even an association of doctors. You might even find weight-lifting organizations. You notice that many sites use the terms "strength training" and "resistance training" when they talk about lifting weights. Now you have more terms to search and more sites to check out. One approach would be to go to the Web site of a reliable organization, such as the American Medical Association, and use its Web site search engine.

Look at your first search. You notice an organization called the American Academy of Pediatrics (AAP). It sounds official so you put the organization in your search box and find its Web site. It's an association of pediatricians. Pediatricians are doctors who treat children and teens. Sounds perfect. You can search the site for weight lifting and strength training. It has a policy that deals with weight lifting and children and teens. It's a little hard to understand, so you print it out, take it to your dad, and have him read it with you.

Because you found information from a reliable source, you are better able to convince your dad that it's OK for you to strength train. He agrees that you can try it out, but only if you train with your coach or gym teacher around. Dad even suggests you show the AAP policy to your coach and gym teacher. He also says maybe you could search the Web a little more to make sure other reliable sources agree with the AAP. You head back to the computer to find weight-lifting associations. They might have information, too.

Did You Hear the One About . . .

Information sent to your e-mail in-box is harder to figure out because you don't know where the information comes from. Did your friend forward you news from a reliable Web site? Did the information even come from a Web site, or did someone playing a big Web practical joke make something up? More often than not, e-mail information that is not personal from the sender is false and incorrect. Pranksters even write e-mails to sound authoritative by claiming they come from someone like a doctor, government official, or important

Wiki What?

One of the most popular Web sites is Wikipedia.org. It's the largest multilingual, free encyclopedia on the Web. Visitors can search more than 7 million articles in 200 languages. During April of 2006 alone, 2.9 million American teens turned to the site for information. Sounds good, right? Not quite.

Millions of volunteers write and edit Wikipedia articles collaboratively, or together. The upside is that the site, using software called Wiki, is easy to use. The downside is that there is no guarantee that the information is accurate. Most articles link to the sources of information authors used for research, but some authors don't do research. The links for other articles go to sites that aren't reliable. Some pages on Wikipedia are one-sided ads for a product. Wikipedia users flag, or report, entries like this, but with millions of articles, some slip through.

Wikipedia is a great place to start a search. You should never rely on information from just Wikipedia, though. Be sure to check out sites that aren't linked to the Wikipedia article. This way, you can make sure that more than just Wiki says it's true.

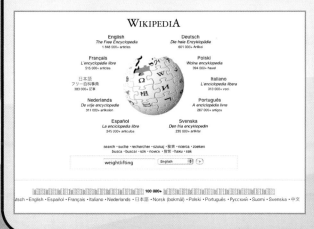

The Wikipedia homepage is a good place to start a search for information, but often the information is unreliable and incomplete. You can find Wikipedia at www.wikipedia.org.

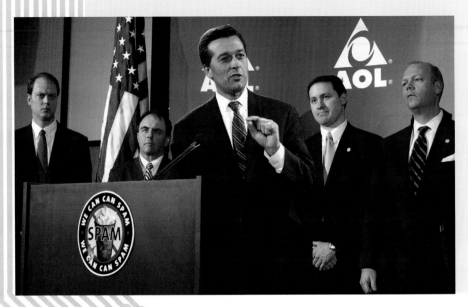

In 2003, the Virginia attorney general announced America's first felony charges for sending illegal e-mail, called spam, over the Internet. The e-mail you get from friends isn't usually illegal, but it is often untrue.

businessperson. Unfortunately, often the person does not even exist, or at the very least, never said what the e-mail claims was said.

Take everything you read in e-mail with a grain of salt. That's an old-fashioned way of saying you should doubt what you read. Check it out right away. Don't forward the e-mail to the people in your address book just because the sender asks you to do that. Even if you don't want to take the time to check something out keep in mind that:

- There is not someone going around major cities removing people's kidneys.
- There is not a single company that tracks the e-mails you send to give you money, gifts, trips, or gift cards.
- There is not a *Guinness World Records* book category for most things received in the mail, so don't send a card to a dying kid who is trying to break that record.
- The girl or boy in the photo doesn't exist or isn't still missing, so don't contact the police with information on his or her disappearance.
- Putting cola in your toilet may or may not get rid of the ring of dirt.

All of this is a way of saying that no matter how much the e-mail might make you sigh "aww," check it before you forward it. If you don't have the time to check it out, delete it. Forwarding hoax e-mails just makes them last longer. Reading e-mails that are untrue makes people take action and waste time. In some cases, you might do more harm than good if you forward information that takes away from a real issue or investigation. Some people might stop reading your e-mails, too, if you constantly forward bad information.

Chapter 3

Get Your Information the Smart Way

With billions of bytes of online information at your fingertips, it's important that you learn to be cyber literate. In order to do that, you must look closely at information. Some of the things to ask yourself when you are trying to decide if information is accurate are:

- Who owns the Web site and put up the information? An individual person? Is he or she an expert? Or is the site owned by a university, government, or professional group? These are more likely to be reliable. Think about who you would ask in real life for information: a coach, a teacher, or a local businessperson. Look for those same kinds of sites online.

This cyber literate student uses the Internet and other sources, such as maps and charts, to find current weather information.

- How did you find the Web site? A search engine will index reliable and unreliable sites. Did you find the site through a link on another site that was very reliable?
- How current or recent is the information on the site? Is information backed up with studies and research? Information can change almost as soon as

If It Makes You Feel Bad, Tell Someone

The Web makes the world bigger. You can find more good stuff, but you can find more bad stuff, too. What do you do when you read or see something that makes you feel uncomfortable?

Stop-Go-Tell

- Stop looking at it.
- Go to a grownup.
- Tell him or her what you saw and where it is.

—Adapted from the Crime Victims' Center of Chester County, PA, Inc.'s flyer "How to Be Cyber-Smart"

Adults can report Web content that is harmful to children and teens at the following sites:

United States:
National Center for Missing and Exploited Children
http://www.cybertipline.com

Canada:
The Canadian Center for Child Protection
English: http://www.cybertip.ca/en/cybertip/
French: http://www.cybertip.ca/fr/cybertip/

it is put on the Web. More recent information is more reliable than old data.

- Are there links to other sites showing similar information? Do the links work? Links that don't work might mean the Web site is old and has not been updated.
- Does the site use data and research from government and scientific studies?
- What is the purpose of the site? Is it selling something, expressing someone's opinion, or talking about both sides of a topic? Does the information make sense or feel right? Ask a grownup if you are not sure.
- Does the Web site look professional, or does it have a lot of mistakes and typos in it? Is there a way to contact the site owner?

Who You Gonna Click? Hoaxbusters!

It might seem impossible to figure out what sites and information are accurate and reliable. Fortunately, there are some Web sites that track other sites and e-mails. They keep lists of sites that are fake and e-mails that are frauds. Start with these sites. They have been online for years and are reliable.

Hoaxbusters at http://hoaxbusters.ciac.org has useful information on Web site and e-mail hoaxes and urban legends. An urban legend is a story that has been around so long that people think it's true just because so many people say it's true.

ScamBusters at http://www.scambusters.org gives information about dishonest e-mails that try to trick you out of your money. You might want to share this Web site with a grownup.

Snopes at http://www.snopes.com is another great site for information on the latest urban legends, hoaxes, and scams going around the Web. It has a huge archive of examples.

The Good, the Bad, but Mostly the Ugly

Along with true and accurate sites on the Web, there are many sites that promote hate, racism, and violence. These sites use bigotry, fear, and false information. Many hate sites make up evidence to support their opinions. Sometimes it is easy to figure out a site is being hateful. Other times, the hate is carefully hidden in the words. Students have stumbled on these sites and used them for reports. They thought the information was accurate. This especially happens with hate sites about historical figures. If a site makes you feel uncomfortable, show it to an adult and talk about it.

Chapter 4

When the WWW Spills into the Real World

How you use the information you find on the Web can affect your life offline. Sometimes it's easy to tell how being cyber literate can affect you. Other times, it's harder to tell. Let's start with the easy to tell: Wikipedia, other study resources, and plagiarism. Plagiarism is when you use someone else's work and take the credit. Web sites such as Wikipedia have a lot of information that some people just use as their own. One author says that plagiarism has quadrupled in the last six years. The Web makes it easier to spot plagiarism, so more people are finding it.

You can get bad grades in school if you plagiarize work. You might even get suspended or expelled from school. True, you might not get caught at first or at all, but if you don't learn how to give credit to other people when you use their ideas and work, it will catch up with you some day. Why take that risk? Do you want to be known as the student who copies people? If you get that reputation, people will no longer trust your work. Then, they might not trust you as a person.

Even the Pros Plagiarize Sometimes

People who were experts in their field and famous writers, such as historian Stephen Ambrose, admitted that they plagiarized at one time. One reporter copied an article from the Internet and gave it to his newspaper to print as his own. Why do people, even famous people, plagiarize? Sometimes they are on a deadline and do it to finish their work in time. They think no one will catch them.

Some people say they didn't even know they plagiarized. They read things over and over and the words stuck in their minds. They didn't realize it when they wrote the same words later in their own work. Unfortunately for them, a reader might point it out. It is plagiarism whether or not you did it on purpose.

How Can I Do What the Pros Can't?

You might think if adults don't know when they plagiarize, how will you ever know? There is one simple thing you can do that will keep you from plagiarizing: give credit where

Rick Bragg *(left)* greets a fan. In 2003, Bragg resigned as a reporter for the *New York Times* after it was discovered that he put his name on an article he didn't write. This is plagiarism, or using someone else's words as your own.

credit is due. This means if you use someone else's work, say so. How do you know if you use someone else's work? Learn to summarize, paraphrase, and quote. The most important thing you can do when you take notes for your own work is to write down where you got the information. Be sure to write who said it, what he or she said it in, and the page number or online URL. (The following is

adapted from http://www.bridgewater.edu/WritingCenter/
manual/paraphrase.htm.)

Summarize: When you summarize something, you rewrite
  it in a shorter form. Summaries are clear and keep the main
  points from the longer work. Don't change the main points,
  and keep it short. You should write where you got the
  main points after the summary. This is called a citation.
  You should also include sources, or where you got your
  ideas, at the end of your work, in a bibliography. The
  bibliography lists all the sources you looked at and read.
  There is a bibliography at the end of this book. Here is
  my citation for this summary: Bridgewater College Writing
  Center (http://www.bridgewater.edu/WritingCenter/
  manual/paraphrase.htm).

Paraphrase: When you paraphrase something, you use
  different words and sometimes change the order of information. Paraphrasing does not make the work shorter. It
  is also not the same as changing a few words here and
  there. You should also cite your source when paraphrasing
  and put the source in your bibliography.

Quote: Quoting someone is the easiest way to use someone
  else's work. You want to use quotes to support your own
  ideas and thoughts. Always use quote marks and the exact
  same wording. You don't want to write that someone said
  something he or she didn't say. It's not accurate or honest.
  Write who said the quote right after you use it.

The Lowdown on Copyright

According to a 2005 report by the Pew Internet and American Life Project, half of all teens have put something online. They have created blogs and Web pages. They have posted artwork, stories, and photographs. They have even posted videos online. Often, they remix someone else's work to create new stuff. What many teens have not done, though, is check out copyright law.

Copyright protects a person's original work. If you use someone else's work in your own, you might be breaking copyright law. If you burn your friend's music CD, you are probably breaking copyright law. Copyright laws vary from country to country, but most share some basic ideas.

Check out these sites to learn more about copyright:

Kids Pages, United States Patent and Trademark Office
http://www.uspto.gov/go/kids

Copyright Kids! Copyright Society of the U.S.A.
http://www.copyrightkids.org

YouTube is one of the most popular Web sites. Videos are posted on the site, many of which use other people's art, words, and music.

Hide and Seek

Hidden ads are much harder to understand than plagiarism, when it comes to how they affect your life. These ads can affect how you think and act, without you even noticing. Everyone knows that television, magazines, radio, and newspapers have advertisements. You also know that there are ads on the Web. Sometimes, though, an ad is disguised to look like a regular Web site with "research." The research is really an opinion. This kind of Web site gives you only the positive side of something. You might use the site to make up your mind about an issue. You might buy something because of what the Web site said and showed. You make a decision without getting all the information. This is not using the Web wisely.

Governments usually don't have as many requirements for Web sites to follow as they do for ads on television. This means that you could see things on the Web that you would never see on television. You might hear things you would not hear on the radio. Television ads cannot show anyone drinking beer and alcohol. The government doesn't allow ads for cigarettes on TV. You won't see people smoking on TV either anymore. This is because studies have shown that ads can convince young people that drinking and smoking are cool. Many popular Web sites show people smoking and drinking. You might start to question the bad things you have heard about drinking and smoking. You could be tempted to drink and smoke.

Chapter 5

Where Will Cyber Literacy Go from Here?

The Internet and Web change every day. Information changes. New Web sites are added. Technology changes, too. Online technology is the tools that help people use computers, the Internet, and the Web. There are new ideas and technology that will make it easier to be cyber literate. Some of these ideas are in the works now. Others have barely been thought of yet.

Many of the ideas already in the works have to do with better search engines. A better search engine would help people be cyber literate. How? First by using spiders that can tell if a page has accurate information, then by ranking more accurate pages higher on your search list. This would help you find the most reliable pages quicker. Less accurate pages would get fewer hits and would show up lower and lower on your search list.

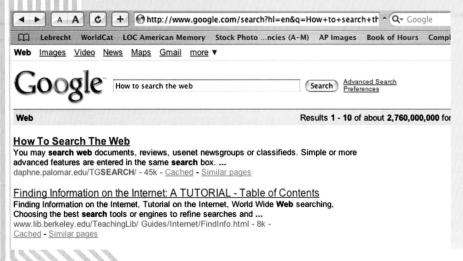

Google is the most popular search engine on the Web. Some day soon, Google and other search engines hope to make it even easier for people to search for information on the Web.

Another way search engines are beginning to change is by making it easier to ask for information. You type keywords now. One search engine lets you type a question, then tries to figure out what you want it to find. This is a very difficult thing for search engines to do. More and more search engines are trying to make is so that people will be able to type a normal sentence to start a search. You won't have to think about keywords or phrases to use. The search engine companies are working on ways to do this and still make the searches accurate.

Copyright Down the Road

More changes are in the works for copyright laws. Millions of teens download music and movies from the Internet. Trying to find a fair way to pay artists but still make files easily available is a challenge. Copyright law has not caught up yet. At some point, the law will be fine-tuned to make it easier to share information, including tunes and movies. Easier to share doesn't mean free, though. The people who make the music and movies need to get money for their work. It's a balance that the law has not quite figured out.

Some people have already made changes in the copyright area. They are at the beginning of a long process, though. Creative Commons is a copyright idea that lets people decide how they want to make their work available. For example, someone could post art and say that it is in the public domain. That's a legal way of saying that anyone can use the work for free, as long as they say where the work came from when they use it.

The copyright laws in the United States and Canada allow people to protect their work for many years. They can charge other people who want to use it. Creative Commons tells people upfront whether work is free to use. Sometimes, people might say their work is free if you are going to use it and not make money. If you use it and make money, though, you might have to pay to use it. For example, you could use a poem in a newsletter that you make for your family. The

Myths and Facts

Myth: Virus and hoax e-mails started in the last five years, as the size of the World Wide Web exploded.

Fact: The first virus e-mails hit in-boxes nearly as soon as the average person started using the Internet at home, work, and school. One of the first virus e-mails was called "Really Nasty Virus" and appeared in 1988. The virus was supposed to attack modems. In 1999, a hoax about a cell phone virus popped up in e-mail in-boxes. There are no known viruses at this time that will destroy cell phone software.

(Sources: http://hoaxbusters.ciac.org/HBHoaxInfo.html#history, http://www.snopes.com/computer/virus/mobile.htm)

Myth: If you use more than one search engine, such as Google.com and Ask.com, to do a search, you will find all the information available on your topic.

Fact: Even if you used a dozen search engines to research some thing, you will not find all the available information on a topic. You won't even find all the information available just on the World Wide Web (WWW). If you use only search engines to find information for a report, you will miss a lot of important information and data. That is why you should always use other sources, too, such as your library catalog to find books about your topic; other databases available through your library that store information and photographs from magazines, journals, and newspapers; and WWW directories of Web sites arranged by topic.

(Source: http://www.vts.intute.ac.uk/detective/thebad.html)

Myth: "Internet" and "World Wide Web" are different words meaning the same thing.

Fact: The World Wide Web is a part of the Internet. If you use the word "Internet" to mean the Web, it would be like calling your tires a bike. The tires are just a part of the whole package. The Internet, or Net, is made up of many subnetworks that share millions of computers and billions of cables. You use different types of software to navigate the subneworks. Each one has its own language, called a protocol. The WWW, or Web, is the largest and most popular Internet subnetwork. You surf the Web with a browser. You use different software and another subnetwork to send e-mail to your friend. Want to burn music and videos? That's more software on yet another subnetwork.

(Source: http://netforbeginners.about.com/cs/technoglossary/f/Faq1.htm)

person who wrote the poem would let you use the poem for free. If you used the poem in a newsletter that you sold, though, the author of the poem might ask you to pay a fee.

Take Note of This

Here's an easy way to take notes. You can do this for information online and offline.

- Make a note about what you read. One note = one idea. Type your note in a word-processing document or write your note on an index card.

- Put information about where you got the note next to it. If it's from the Web, write or type the URL address and the date you saw it. Write the title, the author, and the page number if your note is from a book, magazine, or newspaper.
- Also next to the note, put a P, S, or Q. P stands for "paraphrase," S stands for "summary," and Q stands for "quote."
- Print out the notes if you type them on the computer. Cut the notes into strips. One note on each strip.
- Put the notes in order on a table. Move around the strips or index cards until your ideas make sense. If you typed the notes, you can cut and paste to put them in order.
- Use the notes to make an outline. Use your outline to write your paper. You have all the information you need to give people credit for their work.

What's in Your Future

More important than any technology that will make searches more accurate and files easier to get is how you will change. Your brain is the supercomputer that will help you become cyber literate. Make sure that some changes are on the horizon for you, too.

Work on getting thinking skills that help you figure out if information is accurate. Slow down and spend time carefully reading and looking at Web sites. Check out sites that tell you about hoaxes and hate sites. Be sure to check more than one site for your research. Most important, make sure you use sites that are reliable and authoritative. They are more likely to have the most recent information.

If you do the things in this book to become cyber literate, you will most likely find accurate information. Make sure cyber literacy is one of the tools you use to find the best information. It's a tool that will help you surf the Web wisely now and in the future.

Be cyber literate! Use your thinking skills when you read Web sites. Check out more than one Web site, and use sites that are reliable and authoritative. Be sure to use other sources such as books and magazine articles, too.

Glossary

accurate Correct or true.

affect To act on, change.

authoritative Highly reliable and accurate, based on evidence.

citation (cite) A note that says where you got information that you use in your work.

collaboratively To create something by working or cooperating with others.

cyber literate Able to look at online information with a critical eye to tell if it is reliable and accurate.

cyber world The online World Wide Web.

hit A connection made to a Web site.

hoax Prank or trick.

hypertext markup language (HTML) A computer language used on each WWW page that provides information about how to format the page.

Internet A gigantic computer network that links smaller networks worldwide to provide information to users and let them exchange messages.

interpret To explain and understand.

literate Having skill and knowledge or able to read and write.

meta tag Special HTML coding that tells search engines keywords and ideas on a Web page.

plagiarize To take words and ideas from someone else and use them as your own.

reliable Accurate, dependable, and honest.

reputation The opinions about a person or thing.

World Wide Web (WWW) A system of interlinked documents that appear as Web sites on the Internet.

For More Information

American Library Association
50 East Huron
Chicago, IL 60611
(800) 545-2433
E-mail: library@ala.org
Web site: http://www.ala.org/greatsites
  A national librarians' professional organization with a directory of Web
  sites for kids reviewed and approved by member librarians. Also a page on
  how to tell if you are looking at a great Web site (http://www.ala.org/ala/
  alsc/greatwebsites/greatwebsitesforkids/greatwebsites.htm).

Canadian Media Awareness Network
1500 Merivale Road, 3rd Floor
Ottawa, ON K2E 6Z5
Canada
(613) 224-7721
(800) 896-3342
E-mail: info@bewebaware.ca
Web site: http://www.bewebaware.ca/english/EffectiveOnline.aspx
  Be Web Aware is a Canadian bilingual public-education program on
  Internet safety.

Web Sites

Due to the changing nature of Internet links, Rosen Publishing
has developed an online list of Web sites related to the subject of
this book. This site is updated regularly. Please use this link to
access the list:

http://www.rosenlinks.com/cccs/cyli

For Further Reading

Bennington, Stephen. *All About Computers: Amazing Microchip Machines and Technology*. London, England: Southwater, 2002.

Brimmer, Larry Dane. *The World Wide Web*. Danbury, CT: Children's Press, 2000.

Kazunas, Charnan, and Thomas Kazunas. *The Internet for Kids*. Danbury, CT: Children's Press, 2001.

Pederson, Ted, and Francis Moss. *Internet for Kids*. New York, NY: Price Stern Sloan, 2001.

Roddel, Victoria. *Internet Safety: Kids' Guide*. Morrisville, NC: Lulu.com, 2007.

Sherman, Josepha. *The History of the Internet*. Danbury, CT: Franklin Watts, 2003.

Sommervill, Barbara A. *The History of the Computer*. Mankato, MN: The Child's World, 2006.

Whitcombe, Dan. *Kids' Guide to the Internet*. New York, NY: DK Kids, 2001.

Bibliography

Bausch, Suzie. "Nielsen/NetRatings Announces May U.S. Search Share Rankings." Nielsen/NetRatings. June 20, 2007. Retrieved June 20, 2007 (http://www.nielsen-netratings.com/pr/pr_070620.pdf).

Be Web Aware. "Effective Online Searching." Web Aware/Canadian Media Awareness Network. Retrieved June 1, 2007 (http://www.bewebaware.ca/english/EffectiveOnline.aspx).

Be Web Aware. "Kid-Friendly Sites." Web Aware/Canadian Media Awareness Network. Retrieved June 1, 2007 (http://www.bewebaware.ca/english/KidFriendlySearchEngines.aspx).

Be Web Aware. "Misinformation." Web Aware/Canadian Media Awareness Network. Retrieved June 1, 2007 (http://www.bewebaware.ca/english/misinformation.aspx).

Deal.org/Canadian Mounted Police. "E-Literacy." Retrieved May 31, 2007 (http://www.deal.org/content/index.php?option=com_content&task=view&id=125&Itemid=136).

Franklin, Curt. "How Internet Search Engines Work." How Stuff Works. Retrieved June 2, 2007 (http://computer.howstuffworks.com/search-engine1.htm).

Goodstein, Anastasia. *Totally Wired: What Teens and Tweens Are Really Doing Online.* New York, NY: St. Martin's Press, 2007.

Gurak, Laura J. *Cyberliteracy: Navigating the Internet with Awareness.* New Haven, CT: Yale University Press, 2001.

"How to Be Cyber-Smart." Flyer from the Crime Victim's Center of Chester County, Inc., Chester County, Pennsylvania.

Internet Society. "A Brief History of the Internet." Retrieved May 30, 2007 (http://www.isoc.org/internet/history/brief.shtml#Future).

Internet Society. "Histories of the Internet." Retrieved June 1, 2007 (http://www.isoc.org/internet/history).

Internet World Statistics. "Usage and Population Statistics." Retrieved June 1, 2007 (http://www.internetworldstats.com/stats.htm).

Kelsey, Candace M. *Generation My Space: Helping Your Teen Survive Online Adolescence*. New York, NY: Marlowe & Company, 2007.

Lenhart, Amanda, Mary Madden, and Paul Hitlin. "Teens and Technology." Pew Internet and American Life Project (PIP). July 27, 2005. Retrieved June 1, 2007 (http://www.pewinternet.org/pdfs/PIP_Teens_Tech_July2005web.pdf).

National School Boards Foundation. "Trends Within the Children's Online Industry." Safe & Smart. Retrieved May 28, 2007 (http://www.nsbf.org/safe-smart/trends.htm).

Online Education Database "Research Beyond Google: 119 Authoritative, Invisible, and Comprehensive Resources." October 26, 2006. Retrieved on May 30, 2007 (http://oedb.org/library/college-basics/research-beyond-google#general).

Place, E., M. Kendall, D. Hiom, H. Booth, P. Ayres, A. Manuel, and P. Smith. "Internet Detective: Wise up to the Web." 3rd edition, 2006. Retrieved June 2, 2007 (http://www.vts.intute.ac.uk/detective/index.html).

Snopes.com. "Craig Shergold." April 12, 2007. Retrieved May 29, 2007 (http://www.snopes.com/inboxer/medical/shergold.asp).

Virginia Department of Education. "Report: Guidelines and Resources for Students." Division of Technology and Human Resources, Office of Educational Technology. Richmond, VA. August 13, 2006.

Widener University Wolgram Memorial Library. "How to Do Research." Retrieved June 2, 2007 (http://www3.widener.edu/Academics/Libraries/Wolfgram_Memorial_Library/Need_Help_/How_to_do_Research/486/).

Willard, Nancy E. *Cyber-Safe Kids, Cyber-Savvy Teens: Helping Young People to Use the Internet Safely and Responsibly*. San Francisco, CA: Jossey-Bass, 2007.

Index

About the Author

A computer geek since the mid-1980s when she bought her first Macintosh computer for the price of a used car, Sue Gregson has been surfing the Internet nearly every day since 1994 when "Internet in a Box" first brought the World Wide Web (WWW) into the average American home. Gregson is a writer and editor and the author of more than a dozen nonfiction books for kids. She does her research online and in printed resources such as books, magazines, and newspapers because she knows you need information from various places in order to tell the most accurate story. She has tween and teen sons, and a computer geek husband who surfs the Internet responsibly, too. When she doesn't have her nose glued to a computer screen, Gregson and her family like to explore the history of the Philadelphia area, where they live with a dog, a few fish, and the occasional toad in the sock drawer.

Photo Credits

Cover Les Kanturek; pp. 6, 22, 31 © AP Images; p. 10 Cybergeography.org. Used with permission. p. 11 © Getty Images; p. 12 © 2007 HowStuffWorks; p. 25 © Harry Sieplinga/HMS Images/Getty Images; p. 33 © AFP/Getty Images; p. 41 © DCA Productions/Getty Images.

Editor: Bethany Bryan; **Photo Researcher:** Cindy Reiman